Selected Poems

Volume I

Kelley Shields

BookLeaf
Publishing

India | USA | UK

Made with ❤ on the BookLeaf Publishing Platform
www.bookleafpub.in
www.bookleafpub.com

Dedication

Dedicated to my mother and father, who lived everyday in service to six other human beings and did so with the highest degree of honor to their creative natures. My life choices mirror the practice they made of visualizing, believing and making.

Preface

I told my mother when I was five that my imagination was my best friend. This statement was produced in response to her query of why was I sitting on the curb, swirling street-grit around with a twig: '*What are you doing out there—waiting for your best friend?* She was referring probably to Lorraine, my human best friend, or possibly to my older sibling who I pined for during the hours she was in school.

My response came quickly, as a matter of correction for her enlightenment— '*My best friend is not a person, and I am practicing my letters in the sand. I can write here in the street.*'

The manipulation of words and the beauty, pain, thrill, fear and more that may or may not result from their combination has been my most-consuming pastime for as long as I can remember. I wrote poems by the curb, morbidly fascinated by the understanding that they would disappear when a bicycle, car or foot erased them unwittingly. The fascination I think was that this awareness justified the compulsion I felt to return and create more.

Acknowledgements

I want to acknowledge the endless inspiration provided by the works of Arthur Rimbaud, Rainer Maria Rilke, Virginia Woolf, Simone de Beauvoir, Marcel Proust and Samuel Beckett, to name only a few.

I also extend heartfelt gratitude to Ms. Anita Bennett, my fourth grade teacher, whose genuine appreciation of the poems I wrote for her daily encouraged me to establish a practice of writing. I took to heart her entreaty at the finish of the school year. Her inscription in a journal of my poems she copied over into the book read, 'Keep writing!'

1991. Against the Grain

Even if he were,
the grand he—the one we love and miss
were here
and she, the one who remains
the one whom we love and bear
set the table with staples and adhered paper to the walls
and a wind like wolves' breath
didn't shake the moon rattle the sky stir the stars like
pudding
there would be still
fruit in a bowl sometime that doesn't get eaten soon
enough.

The color brown. The drunk odor. The cavalry of
pinpoint flies.
Righteous diligent purposeful menacing flies.

Reindeer, bow your head
feel the human search.
Bull, charge the hallways of my house.
Find me under my bed, run me down, run me through.
If your coat of short coarse hair
was dragged against its grain after a kill

would your follicles still be sensitive?
I say so.

2008. I Can't Wait for Wanting

Lift then burrow.
Find then lose.
Shift then stutter
and bellow it out like barks in a ragged dog fight without
rules or refs.

My starlight wishes for a shine that blinds you or others
enough
to say all the things that used to be said often to me;
things I would smile after hearing and appreciate with
gratitude
as if I were gifted, and undeservedly at that.
As if I were the lucky recipient of something belonging
to another
so I for sure sent thanks back up there, right to the
source
that gave me so much.
I never wanted for anything
except a quiet loving place.

I found no such one place
there were instead many raucous wild places
and wild times to silence the cleaving, heaving,

massacre-severed claw times;
home was not as bad as that except,
that memory is a young child
scared and inexperienced, so
it shudders when others barely shift.

I can't wait for wanting again this time
for the words and thinking we once shared
which was the more valuable of everything.
There was too little in the end,
too short a time
before it all crumpled.
And it did not have to,
because what was real was valuable
and vice versa.

What was invaluable was not real
so, there were no losses really
worth throwing good away.

But, you did. You threw everything away.

1987 - 1993. Little Works

REVIVE

Irrigate the unused
Skin on my face
There are lines of
Vegetal roots
Descend deep my whole
Soul is the pool which
Feeds their flowering

MUD

Let me be slick mud.
Let me be velvet moss on a cliff
so high barely a wing
sets down to rest.
Let loose rained earth glimmer
with minerals, shine like it is glazed
let it seep into cracks
let seeds there fall, let trees there grow.
Let my surface be as a mirror. Let me be
other than human. At last simply
a part of this ground earth.

FLOAT

Sway the terra

Cup this bristling admonition.
Leap unbounded the triangles of earth
and lift then, undaunted.
Move the braced in soul and
Free the shackled breath.
Let mist saturate a tank of rocks.
Let gallons collect.
Let finally, these stones float.

END TO BEGIN
Where do I step?
The oval beneath as are infinity
there are alleys that
carousels turn like
always at the end it
becomes the starting point.

HAIKU of GONE
Slab sleeping.
Side on flat lie.
Flat side red.
Blue palor up.
Last breath gone.
No more movement.

MAJESTY DANCE
When day and night touch

their majesty dance
it robs me blind of my attention
to will it otherwise i cannot
while the dance is danced
I am the awe struck audience
and the standing ovation.
Standing ovated
over the crest of the hill
the dancers sweep, they dip
then, one remains.

SINTER FELL

Find my wing under that stone
bring it her e to my side, beside my self;
a worm can regrow its other half
when sliced.

If there is memory
we can expect regeneration
of moments to occur as called upon.
Don't recall pain, is good advice.
What is not recalled did not occur?
No, will not occur again; until the next time only
that enough feathers fall to lame a wing.

2010. Underfull

A ladle and a fork poke through a vessel-bag
a satchel, a bladder that holds the life stuff of you plus
me,
together we've walked so many miles
and across so many places
trifling some of the time but mostly
building huts and foraging and wearing paths
through growth
struck a good deal of the time in the face
with a branch released not on purpose mostly
by one of us, but sometimes this way
backwards, at the other
a mere step behind.

Gone, you are not thankful I am
all the times I have screamed at the air
and whined into nobody's ear while crying
through my teeth about how hard
something was as if because of you—
now, always really, but now I really know
today this minute I feel more than ever
how less hard everything is because of you.

Oh, the favor of greeting skin that knows

each other, the remembering holds of
arms that know each other, the graceful bends and folds
into each other's sections and empty spots—
all of this has been gifted me
never lonely, not really. I've known love
true love all along
walking this life of mine.

2011. Sanctity

I pull some flesh across my face
your arm or under-wrist, smooth
and cradle three maybe four fingers
in a few of mine, in this way
time wrangles around.
I while it away with you
attempting to use
it with purpose.

What if we just walk around for years
and don't make any plans other than what we hold
and take, like breath from each other's mouths
or skin from under our nails
dug in from gripping,
I liked life that way.

Hours were weeks
weeks became years—
it seems I had more of that time
than I do now; now is so much
here, all the time.

I laid down beside you
and I never got up.

2010. Beating Air

Hanging a hold with pounding fists
seeking to displace some latent memory
now settled like so much dust
of where we were
these fists are not at all like earlier
matched with scared—the flavor of thrill
and being the loathed trophy it was
care was fully affected to return it to its proper spot
that no notice would be taken
of anxious millimeters off the needle's register,
of its' always place.

Don't flaunt your fears or your wants;
remain unknown, unheard—
this I knew and yet I stumbled
and became suspended in some kind of space,
a distance of hold
like the gulls above my girls once,
all the flailing feathered wings
I shrank from and quaffed, in the same action,
the love-drenching which soaked
me in the distance I put between me and them,
a deliberate distance like extending a page
from blurring in closeness;

an act of keen knowing that
feeling apart from
will increase, automatically want,
dangling our desires before our eyes.

We are all jealous, hungry children.
You, perhaps more jealous than most
behave so thickly; like trying to drizzle cold honey
always looking out of lack's window.
I concede you must have often been without
and so, I invented filling that void.
I was swollen with want to do this for you.

Instead, my thoughts of you are beating air.
Unlucky me, that they are not feathered wings.

2008. No Breath for Me Without Knowing Yours

Call it what you want
trace it to something, anything
but nothing will explain what breath not taken in feels
like.

Nothing can define or capture
what air without oxygen feels like,
collapsing soft tissue pockets for its lack
my lungs not providing
through the deficit of what was not provided them
vital life sustaining elements to the rest of me.

Were you available, breath would still be flowing
as if I were really alive.

2008. Once and Ago, Now Too Also

Never a time there was and wasn't both
it seems we were always this at the same time,
filling and emptying equally
each other's basins and inlets, bays and waterfalls.
I fell into you hard
harder than most not concrete not earth's boulder hard
rather, fully collapsed and given-over hard.
Into you
I became
a different me, so quickly
so early.

I had been waiting by some edge
lesser knowing this truth, more wondering what was
next
already quite released from the beginning of early
woman-ness
exploring still foraging
pretending to be finding
my way and the means to fill this regular hunger
of being in Living's World.
I was very slim beyond body lithe,
slim in here-ness; I, fully Me, was not yet.

I yet needed to come
through to this side
and
you needed to come
through me
to show me, Me.

The freest I've ever been that night, you know it
as if you were present at the moment
of my release from containment.
You knew me as no one else ever will
ballast to a list of this magnitude provided by my
knowing
without knowing how
that I've known you forever and always will.

                        Light was moon
only then purple after long blackness
whitened by pastina stars while bliss was mine.
After the running
and the cartwheels
and the ballet through lacey foam
unfettered, utterly—no ties, no rules, no matter but ours
—

we articulated that No existence Was
save mine, yours, the earth's breath, the pillow sand and
the blanket sky

of that bed, night.

Heaven continued to layer like sublime icing
as I drifted in and out of Eden;
you atop me
you beneath me
you beside me
me, curled into you.
Us, breathing strong and full
then misted then subtle in and out of sleep
in and out of wanting to reclaim a mortal life due with
dawn.

In orange-blue swaths across the field of my cat-caring
slits
I peeked and saw day standing above me demanding its
cost.
Two nuns glanced over their shoulders at so much skin
all of the curves;
the hills up and down of my hips into waist into ribs
against the landscape of your high plain chest
sloping down and in scooping out a velvet valley
your abdomen its hollow holding my head so perfectly.
Forever I wanted to leave my face there and breathe in
you, always you
I believed forever and without end.

As quickly as they discerned our forms
their eyes scattered like embarrassed girls
and buried themselves up to their necks, those eyeballs,
in the sand
contemplating their reluctant spirited walk
perhaps aware that their choices left them with less
and us with a magnificence beyond more, at least at that
moment.

2008. What It Was

Bright lights and bubbles, then white water and spills
into gorges on the ride you were tall enough to board.
And it raced and we turned our insides out like springs
each coil inward spiraling out of the last outer rim
that our edges had tipped over.

Falling in
leaning on
smiling at
laughing with
smelling lovely
holding torrents
tasting salt
finding roofs and valleys,
like painting pink glass
with a weird slippery seal.

In case you forgot what it was,
you were there,
you were smiling,
you had a good time.

2008. Given This

Finger and leaf through my hair
like pages of the letters you wrote
and trace my lips;
you do this and I quake but
asking you to do it more
would make
it less.

Anything often makes it less—
the reverse riddle
more is less is more.
Given this I think I'll ask for none
so I can have the most
of you
and of them.

Strike the bell for stopping
break the flow that carries
stinging beauty and love, pure energy
away from where I can feel it.

Damn it and clog it
so it pools around me

in case in asking for less
I cannot feel more.

1994. Interred

Season the seasonal the seasoning
Season of the interred interred
Blurred my face that dirt I bury
My living heart my living mouth
That delivers air or did, once
To my lung + 1 = lungs.

This dirt did crawl did leap
Into my mouth fill the cavity the cavern
The cave hollowed out like a whale's
Open mouth
Like Pinnochio I can't be trusted to tell all truths?
I wish to tho'. I wish to with
Stars extra amounts of emphasis.
I wish to with exclamation points.
I resist.

After the gullables,
After the inflections,
I gather up fallen bings
Dropped cherries that are sourer
Than sweet
And I avoid the pits.

1995. Carlisle's Bundle

Jung yoo Jung Loo
Ling chun Yat dir

Sweep over any of the no way
I ain't gonna' do it.
When I sat in closets it
was for the too sound
soft muffle and defurring that I'd do.
That blanket still bald covered me enough
the door open one inch ajar only
kept me just a little there.

I hid from them
so they wouldn't find me?
Maybe they wouldn't look.
Maybe I wasn't there.
Maybe I'm not here.

The coils lead to Rome
all roads travel away from home.
Don't outstretch an arm
and don't pave a sidewalk
I won't be coming back.

2010. Infernal Lament

Running circles around
my own feet that purge
along with my soul
me, from a balanced place
into and through the fire
ringing truth and choice
is the seldom shadow that once
belonged sensibly, it felt, to my impression.

What is my impression now,
with these actions that describe only some
of the steps I took?

Shadow, judge me not from these alone,
there are so many others that equal me in total.
How comfortably you perch on the branch
that is not olive;
teeth clamping down
not on haste and bile's mean exit
rather on my cupped hand, extended with a trembled
asking.

You must be cavernous inside
to hold this much.

Imagine the vastness of love and grace
that could flood that place were it not
so full and bone dry.

2009. Silver Swim

Silverfish do not have fins,
their million insect legs
swim a glide that does not match walking at all.

Way back in the beginning of us, the Saccharina ate
perfectly
up to the edges of ink on several mislaid drawings.
Remaining was lace only of marks he made
which was very much perhaps, more beautiful
for the absence
of the structure
on which
the marks were laid.

Like on me, the marks he made, his imprint is more
beautiful
without the beginnings that he made them on.
The used-to-be structure that mocks and derides his
giving effort
his total concentration,
his complete union
with the art of loving me.

I stammer without speaking:

We don't make the tides;
the earth and moon are in collusion.
Puncturing through the sky like a finger through latex
the moon points its power, its pull, at the center of me
and to this all bodies of water obey.
Without choice, my body responds.
I am in a pull that there is resistance to.

I am full in the gravity
of what is indicated,
of what is known by him
but won't be spoken by me.

2009. Anticipation

It's so long ago
I don't remember missing really
and yet, this second, twitching the evidence is, my body
recalls.
Your face might emerge from a pile
of heads at different tallness
blends of caucasian latin asian black
spew from below the blends result
through bars
my sight line a bit above their rising
each bar breaking my breath and hope
the stair edge finally reveals like
a curtain retracted what the banister kept blind
each time I hoped and held.

Not you. Not you again. Neither, nor, nope no,
no, no.
I keep looking though as if there is a reason to.
You are not coming.
Now I'll let go.

2005. Nymph

Grainy light thin and grey not opaque
subdues his outline raucous in her mind
impatient in her mouth to sip with her bottom lip
from the tip of his longest finger
to the round of his shoulder.

Always the light relaxes what could otherwise be violent
not senseless with danger attached
just primary, basic, uninterrupted, unmannered
not taught to keep one hand on the lap
while the other feeds
him to her.

Again tonight then again tomorrow night
then again the next
without end
this inefficiency of replenishment
like gas to an engine
food to a body
water to a potted plant
is the only welcome one she thinks
all others, mere annoyances of redundancy.

She curls then unfolds her toes for grip

across the tops of his feet
while standing and leaning into his front
soon they will lie and turn and turn like on a spit,
the fire will be their own burning.

1989. Jeterpear

Triangle the sweaty nut
the nervous nut
the jittering wretch
that runs about the room
sitting in a chair
fingering its greasy salt hair;
wash the floor beneath
its feet
will be lifted up
by the knees
and the mop
will lash up softly
some grime across
its ankle.

A pear for lunch on the Great Plains?
Owe'in our lives to a
conqueror of many, hail
hail the seafaring landlord.

Is that a flag the rat notes?
I've no flag,
I run in circles or squares
and owe nothing to nobody.

2009. Round Hold

They roll out of your throat the binds you use;
you rumble it up knowing fully it kills me.
This is the way my captivation is strung
leaving me knotted and knotted and bitten.
You round it into my eardrums beating like the fists
of an excited infant without language to speak
his thrill as he takes in her trill
all violet and lavender, the syllables
she stops and starts staring over his body
applying her care; this mother's look defines
devotion and protection that come from a cellular,
patterned place.

A reaction of this sort
involuntary
overcomes me, your round voice it rolls over me.
All the words not even some of the words,
all the sounds not even some of the sounds
even the empty space of breath in between
vowels and consonants linking arms as if dancing,
advancing movements that speak smug steps
over the surface of my skin, they travel
up then down, up then down, up and down, my skin—
on my face they seem to begin

spilling over my jaw, dropping to my throat
dividing across my clavicles
spidering through my chest, all wiry and lacy. Metallic
and icy
combining again as a gorge to my stomach, draining to
my root.

Spray splashes up to my ears, speckling the rims only—
the irritation of an insufficient swell
holds me, holds me round in string
and other bondages it seems, much less easily broken.

I am held round in your voice to which I willingly
submit.
I soften and listen waiting with open seams all over
to feel this expansive restriction again.

2008. Magnetic Fields

Get going into me, tackle then lift and walk
a far way straight down this road ahead, wherever it
may go—throw
me over your shoulder, over that boulder up a bit longer
the weight won't be so bad
you are stronger—like what you see in me and like—
than you think I am reckless and I am.

It feels good
to run so forward, so fast this way, eyes closed.
I walk with my face in books
crossing streets from guts
like blind bugs and moles
finding their way all albino in blackness
I let my edges indicate when it is ok to bound out
never looking up.

I crossed you this way and was struck.
I crossed you in error.

My outline was so buzzy, so busy with
your electric plus my electric plus
the core's magnetic plus
the possibility of your many fragile edges;

the cuticles around your nail beds.

The small and the grand at once
I was an electron and a mountain both
while around you—a monolith scattering interference,
obscuring the fractions of clarity
I might have otherwise perceived.

Nerves and scared are racing;
forward is my singular thrill of movement.
Slow offers yawns,
backwards can't be abided
and,
meandering loses interest as often as it sometimes
entertains.

I am not patient. It is thoroughly against my nature.
Do not ask me to be.

2008. Rend and Bear

Warbling in the cavity where pumping generally
animates the likes of me that walks around—
now much more hollow than registers from the outside,
there is a rattle rattle quake
the same caliber as the first time
I tasted the salt of your mouth;
this quake is quite different tho',
being an echo only of the calamity rent to bear.

Headlong into the push and pull of thrill
and fast faster moving with the swell
all or nothing sense was interrupted by with and also
in my mind in my hope disturbing not one bit
everything of value to me, to either you, as well.

For me knowance never held the possibility of damage
and action never held the discipline of possibilities at all.
Like an albatross thermaling, coasting blissful respite
stretches
of rejuvenation on high I was flying, too
with bird's eyes as well as wings the view
lacking scope of the distance down,
of the hardness looming beneath such height.

With and also seemed possible in theory.
With and also should be possible in practice.
I wonder still if the expression of it can be lived.

In my mind a danger didn't exist
to feel the same thing
twice
while divided in two
at once.

I walk about as-if,
though much emptier in the spot
where soaring matchness had too briefly filled me
and,
I can't even let you know, as you won't let me tell you.

If I could touch just the tip
of one finger, if I could brush against a sleeve,
if I could glance the shortest gaze with understanding
back,
I imagine braving a dive in again
aware this time of the extreme depth beneath me.
A knowing of this kind must indeed be rare
its essence too exquisite to be ordinary;
too extra-ordinary to be missed.

The join of my ribs at the angle's smallest opening

first posted the caution I was approaching;
it hurt and was lovely equally.
Your skin warm on mine,
now the time long, quite past still recalls
--awe, the persistence of memory
--the torrent flowing in.

To give back precisely what I received
plus double-more from that moment,
I imagine doing almost anything,
if it would convince you of the purity of my heart.

Realizing what might be lost,
like a diver for pearls my breath holds long
and often.
Without an exhale to relax into,
there are no bubbles
describing my care for you.

www.ingramcontent.com/pod-product-compliance
Lightning Source LLC
LaVergne TN
LVHW010916200726
843509LV00013B/1964